Tiger Woods

ABDO
Publishing Company

3900 MAIN STREET
ROWLETT, TX 75088

A Big Buddy Book
by **Sarah Tieck**

VISIT US AT
www.abdopublishing.com

Published by ABDO Publishing Company, 8000 West 78th Street, Edina, Minnesota 55439.

Printed in the United States.

Coordinating Series Editor: Rochelle Baltzer
Contributing Editors: Heidi M.D. Elston, Megan M. Gunderson, Marcia Zappa
Graphic Design: Maria Hosley
Cover Photograph: AP Photo: Peter Morrison
Interior Photographs/Illustrations: AP Photo: AP Photo (page 22), Elise Amendola (page 17), Chuck Burton (page 22), Rob Carr (page 19), Damian Dovarganes (pages 23, 25), Bob Galbraith (pages 10, 19), Alastair Grant (page 21), Lenny Ignelzi (page 5), David J. Phillip (page 19), Ed Reinke (page 13), Eric Risberg (page 11), Lynne Sladky (page 15), Ted S. Warren (page 19); Getty Images: Doug Benc (page 8), AFP/Timothy A. Clary (page 5), Ken Levine (page 7), David McNew (page 29); Photos.com (page 26).

Library of Congress Cataloging-in-Publication Data;

Tieck, Sarah, 1976-
  Tiger Woods / Sarah Tieck.
     p. cm. -- (Big buddy biographies)
  Includes index.
  ISBN 978-1-60453-127-5
  1. Woods, Tiger. 2. Golfers--United States--Biography--Juvenile literature. I. Title.

GV964.W66T54 2009
796.352092--dc22
   [B]
                              2008009364

Tiger Woods

Contents

A Golf Hero

Tiger Woods is a famous athlete. He is one of the most successful golfers ever!

Over the years, Tiger has set records and won many prizes for golf. He has won all of the majors. Tiger is famous for doing these great things at a young age.

Tiger won the Masters Tournament for the first time in 1997. At 21, he was the youngest person to win the special green Masters jacket.

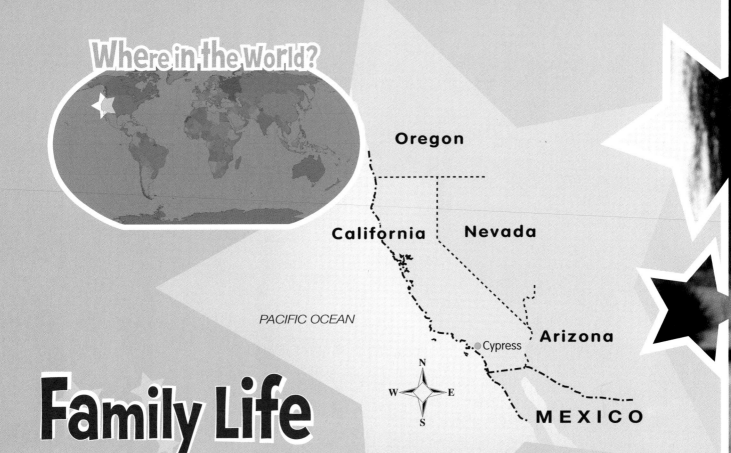

Where in the World?

Oregon

California

Nevada

PACIFIC OCEAN

Cypress

Arizona

MEXICO

N
W E
S

Family Life

Tiger Woods was born on December 30, 1975, in Cypress, California. His parents are Earl and Kultida Woods.

Tiger has three older **siblings**. Kevin and Earl Jr. are his brothers. His sister's name is Royce.

Tiger's mother is from Thailand. His father is from the United States.

Earl wrote two books about his relationship with Tiger. They are Training a Tiger and Playing Through.

Tiger's parents originally named him Eldrick. Later, his father **nicknamed** him "Tiger" after a family friend. The name stuck! At age 21, Tiger **legally** changed his nickname to his real name.

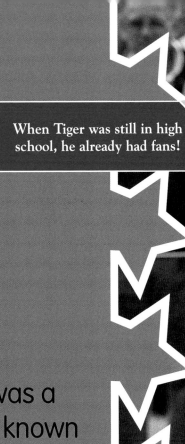

When Tiger was still in high school, he already had fans!

Young Master

Tiger began golfing when he was a very small child. He first became known for his golf skills at age two! At that time, Tiger **putted** against well-known **comedian** Bob Hope on television.

Tiger practiced hard when learning to play. His work paid off. He won many **amateur** honors. Young Tiger's golf skills amazed people!

When Tiger was five years old, he was featured in *Golf Digest* magazine.

Earl taught Tiger to swing a golf club. They began practicing in the family's garage when Tiger was young. After Tiger became a professional, they continued to play together.

In 1994, Tiger won the U.S. Amateur Championship. This allowed him to play in his first Masters Tournament in 1995. He was just 19 years old!

As an amateur, Tiger became known for his skills on the golf course.

In 1984, Tiger won the Junior World Golf Championships for the first time. He won this event five more times.

In 1991, Tiger became the youngest winner of the U.S. Junior Amateur Championship. He also won in 1992 and 1993. Tiger is the only person to win this event three times!

Going Pro

Tiger became a **professional** golfer in 1996. In 1997, Tiger won the Masters Tournament. This was the first **major** he won. Tiger beat the other players by 12 strokes. This set a record!

Many people say Tiger helped draw new fans to the game of golf. Tiger's fans are often colorful and spirited!

Did you know...

Tiger has made 18 holes-in-one! He was six years old the first time he hit one.

In 2000, Tiger won the U.S. Open at Pebble Beach in California. He beat the other players by a record 15 strokes!

As a **professional**, Tiger has won many golf events. His list of wins includes all four **majors**. He has won some of them more than once!

Tiger is the youngest player to win 50 Professional Golfers' Association (PGA) **titles**! He was also named PGA Player of the Year several times.

Major Wins

Tiger was the first African American to win a **major championship**. And, he is the only golfer to hold all four major **titles** at the same time! He has won 14 majors total.

Masters Tournament – 4 wins
(1997, 2001, 2002, 2005)

U.S. Open – 3 wins
(2000, 2002, 2008)

British Open – 3 wins
(2000, 2005, 2006)

PGA Championship – 4 wins
(1999, 2000, 2006, 2007)

The final round of the U.S. Open is always played on the third Sunday in June.

The Masters is held at the Augusta National Golf Club in Georgia.

The PGA Championship is the final major of the golf season. So, its nickname is "Glory's Last Shot."

The British Open is sometimes played at the Royal and Ancient Golf Club of St. Andrews in Scotland.

A Hard Worker

Some of Tiger's skill is natural talent. But, he works hard to sharpen his abilities. Many days, Tiger spends hours exercising and training with coaches.

Tiger often arrives on the golf course early in the morning. He likes to practice before it gets busy.

100

Role Models

Tiger has many role models. Basketball player Michael Jordan is one. Tiger also looks up to golfer Charlie Sifford.

Tiger's most important role model is his father. Earl was Tiger's first golf teacher. And, he was often seen on the golf course when Tiger played.

When Earl died in 2006, Tiger was very sad. He said his father was his best friend.

Basketball star
Michael Jordan and
Tiger are friends.

Tiger had a statue built to honor his father
at the Tiger Woods Learning Center.

A Family Man

Tiger is a husband and a father. He married Elin Nordegren on October 5, 2004.

Family is important to Tiger and Elin. They have a daughter named Sam Alexis Woods. She was born on June 18, 2007.

Sam and Elin often attend golf events with Tiger.

Wyoming

SWEDEN

UNITED STATES

New York

California

Florida

Sweden

INDIAN OCEAN

In addition to homes around the world, Tiger has a large boat called *Privacy*. He keeps it in Florida.

Tiger and his family live in Florida. They have homes in California, New York, Sweden, and Wyoming. And, they continue to purchase homes in new places.

27

Buzz

Tiger enjoys using his money to help others. He works with the Tiger Woods Learning Center. Also, he plans to **expand** the Tiger Woods Foundation. Both of these organizations help children.

Tiger says he will play golf for as long as he can do his best and win. Some say that Tiger will be a billionaire by 2010. He would be the first **athlete** to accomplish this!

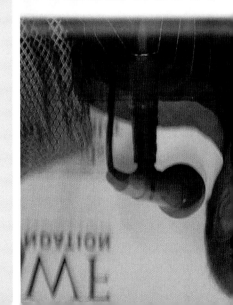

EARL WOODS

TIGER WOODS

Tiger and his father started the Tiger Woods
Foundation in 1996. It helps kids accomplish
their goals and reach their dreams.

Snapshot

⭐ **Name**: Tiger Woods
⭐ **Birthday**: December 30, 1975
⭐ **Birthplace**: Cypress, California
⭐ **Homes**: California, Florida, New York, Wyoming, Sweden
⭐ **Started golfing**: Before age two
⭐ **Turned professional**: 1996
⭐ **Majors won**: Masters Tournament, U.S. Open, British Open, PGA Championship

Important Words

amateur (A-muh-tuhr) an athlete who competes for pleasure instead of for money.

athlete a person who plays sports.

championship a game or a match held to find a first place winner.

comedian a person who uses funny talk and actions to make people laugh.

expand to make larger.

legal based on or allowed by law.

major any of the four important golf games that happen every year. These are the Masters Tournament, the U.S. Open, the British Open, and the PGA Championship.

nickname a name that replaces a person's real name.

professional (pruh-FEHSH-nuhl) working for money rather than for pleasure.

putt a golf stroke made to cause a ball to roll in or near the hole.

sibling a brother or a sister.

title a first-place position or championship.

Web Sites

To learn more about Tiger Woods, visit ABDO Publishing Company on the World Wide Web. Web sites about Tiger Woods are featured on our Book Links page. These links are routinely monitored and updated to provide the most current information available.

www.abdopublishing.com

Index